Poetic Messages
Inspired by the
Holy Spirit

RUTH E. DOWNER

Trilogy Christian Publishers
A Wholly Owned Subsidary of Trinity Broadcasting Network
2442 Michelle Drive
Tustin, CA 92780

For information, address Trilogy Christian Publishing
Rights Department, 2442 Michelle Drive, Tustin, Ca 92780.
Trilogy Christian Publishing/ TBN and colophon are trademarks of Trinity Broadcasting Network.

For information about special discounts for bulk purchases, please contact Trilogy Christian Publishing.

Manufactured in the United States of America

10 9 8 7 6 5 4 3 2 1

Library of Congress Cataloging-in-Publication Data is available.

ISBN 978-1-64773-817-4 (Print Book)
ISBN 978-1-64773-818-1 (ebook)

Contents

Foreword..9
Introduction...10

Part One: Love

Becoming Love..13
Be Still 14
Boundless 15
Change 16
Child 17
Clock 18
Corridor 19
Date 20
Dream 22
Ever After 23
Faith 24
Father of All 25
Filter 26
Flower 27
Fruit of the Spirit 28
Grace and Mercy 30
Hallelujah 31
Home Sweet Home 32
Hummingbird 33
I Can 34

I Love You 35
Keepsake 36
Kiss 37
Love Can Be 38
Love God…Love People 39
Love Her 40
Love Him 42
Love Songs 44
Lovely Venue 45
Next to You 46
Promises 47
Share 48
Supreme 49
The Golden Rule 50
Upon a Rock 51
You Are 52

Part Two: Encouragement

Anew You 54
Another Day 55
Ask 56
Bible 57
Calling 58
First Hour 59
Gift 60
God Knots 61
Grace 62
Heaven's Door 63
His Name 64
Host 65
Home 66
I Lack Nothing 68
I Wait for You, Lord 69

I See 70

Mirror 71

Never Strays Away 72

Old Made New 73

Prayers 74

Road Map 75

Salt & Light 76

Shadow 77

Sharpen 78

Soul Print 79

Sweet Eternity 80

Sun, Moon, & Stars 81

Stones & Butterflies 82

Today 84

Wildest Dreams 85

Part Three: Long Suffering

Amends 87

Angels & Demons 88

Apostle 89

Beatitudes 90

Bite 91

Captive 92

Cross 93

Dance 94

Dark Pathways 95

Deliver 96

Devil's Brew 97

Ego 98

Enduring 99

Freedom 100

Glory 101

Heart 102

Hope 103
Humble Heart 104
Indeed 105
Like Jesus 106
More 107
Sin No More 108
Soar 109
Stop, Drop, and Pray 110
Thorns 111
Wait 112

Part Four: Truth

Abide 114
Atone 115
Behavior 116
Beware 117
Christian 118
Done 119
Fear Not...120
Flee 121
Flesh 122
Grow 123
King 124
Noah 125
Oneness 126
Open Your Eyes 127
Overflow 128
Poke Around 129
Priceless 130
Reconciled 131
Righteousness Sake 132
Rock 133
Saved 134

Suffering 135
The Way 136
There Goes I 137
Thou Art 138
Three Hearts 139
Treasures 140
Two Sins 141
Truth 142
Understanding 143
Warfare 144
What Is Right 145
Wisdom 146
What Pleases Him Will Please You Too 147
Words 148

Conclusion...149
Acknowledgements...150
Bibliography..151

Foreword

Dear Reader,

How do you paint a picture of our savior's love, wisdom, and guidance through words? With all of the love in her heart this is what my precious friend and sister, Ruth, has done on the pages of this book.

While being inspired by our Lord and Savior, Ruth has taken the wisdom given to her through many hours of study, prayer, and meditation. She has transformed it into messages of love, hope, and redemption that only God can provide.

I know the depth of wisdom and love that is received by anyone who is fortunate enough to spend time with Ruth, because I am her best friend and sister in Christ and have been for over thirty years. Ruth has an empathetic sense of knowing that can only be described as a gift from God. She does not take this gift lightly and is in constant awareness of the responsibility placed upon those who share God's word.

As you read through the sentiments and words of love shared in this book by Ruth, you will see a heart dedicated to God and all He has for us, a heart whose only desire is to reach hearts in need of His comfort.

With God's Love,
Julie A. Wiginton,
BSN, RN

Introduction

. . . .

I love the Father, the Son, and the Holy Spirit with all my heart, soul, and mind. No words can truly express how grateful I am to share in the Holy Spirit's supernatural divinity. A divine help that has inspired me to write these poetic messages. Through these poems, the Holy Spirit is relating to us in ways that transcend love, encouragement, long sufferings, and truth, all the while reminding us of the power, grace, and mercy of the heavenly Father. I carry these messages with me as I eat, sleep, and breathe. And with that, I write from my heart to yours.

I often say, "There's a scriptural solution to every problem." So, the next time you find yourself in fear or pain remember that life here is not without suffering. It's only here with Jesus that our lives are not in vain. I pray these Spirit-filled messages continue to walk with you through this life and into eternity.

thank you, God,
for patience
when my faith
was not clear
as I wavered
through the years
now that I know You
I know what to do

and that includes
listening
when You tell me
what to do…
my heart is overflowing
with Your messages
to share
and I'll wait with
bated breath
until the next
assignments here

being confident of this very thing, that He who has begun a good work in you will complete it until the day of Jesus Christ.

Philippians 1:6 (NKJV)

PART ONE:

Love

Becoming Love ~

love is someone
we become…
it's not just for
the ones we love…
can we find
the silver lining
even when it's hiding?
I want to love
like Jesus and
I pray that you
do too and loving
thy neighbor is
what He said to do

You shall love your neighbor as yourself.

Matthew 22:39 (ESV)

Be Still ~

. . . .

open the Bible
and start…
God's word
unlocks the heart…
no better place
to be…than
spending time
with the King
Be Still and Feel His Presence
read the Psalms
get to know
His songs
meet Him
face to face…
God's way
teaches faith
His amazing grace
saves our place
Be Still and Feel His Presence

Be still, and know that I am God; I will be exalted among the
nations, I will be exalted in the earth!

Psalm 46:10 (NKJV)

Boundless ~

divine
unlocked
Thy boundless abyss…
all creatures made
for Thee…
behold, Thy saw it
was all very good
Thou might enjoy
beings set free…

ye sees wisdom's
divine nature
rejoice in Thy
that lives
and soon one day
ye meets divine
in boundless eternal bliss

Then God saw everything that he had made, and indeed it
was very good.

                                        Genesis 1:31 (NKJV)

Change ~

Jesus Christ
changes
lives

through
Him
sin no
longer
wins…

crucified
with
Christ
faithful
in His
love

I have been crucified with Christ; it is no longer I who live, but Christ lives in me; and the life which I now live in the flesh I live by faith in the Son of God, who loved me and gave Himself for me.

Galatians 2:20 (NKJV)

Child ~
. . . .

I am a child of God
Holy Spirit
lives in me
the evil one
cannot take
Holy Spirit
away from me
Thank You Jesus
Thank You Lord
for blessing me
my heart
longs for You
day and night
I dare not
wake or sleep
tonight
without
holding
onto You tight
I am a Child of God

I will be a Father to you, and you shall be My sons and daughters, Says the Lord Almighty.

2 Corinthians 6:18 (NKJV).

Clock ~

. . . .

the grandfather
clock
is the
heartbeat
of the house...
tick-tock
tick-tock
the clock chimes
one to noon...
there's something
special about
the chime that
talks to you...
the next time
that you hear
tick-tock
tick-tock...
remind yourself
to stop
and thank
God for
sweet time

Teach us to number our days, that we may gain a heart of
wisdom.

Psalm 90:12 (NIV)

Corridor ~

Lord help me
look to you
for courage
and strength
while walking
through Your corridor
to life that has
no length…
reminding me
to keep You
directly in
my sight
I daydream
of eternity a place
You've made
for me where everything
is perfect a place I long to be

"Let not your heart be troubled; you believe in God, believe also in Me. In My Father's house are many mansions' if it were not so, I would have told you. I go to prepare a place for you. And if I go and prepare a place for you, I will come again and receive you to Myself; that where I am, there you may be also. And where I go you know, and the way you know."
John 14:1-4 (NKJV)

Date ~

it's never too late to go on a date with Jesus
all those years
unnerving fears
resisting
a date with
the perfect mate...
so, I went on
a date with
Jesus...
we worshiped
all day
and through
the night as
He held
me tight
and brought
to life
a love
hidden deep
in the depths
of my soul...
a love so
sweet, so warm
so true
resistance

was through...
fears they still come
so, I cling to
His love
and go on a date
embracing my fate
it's never too late to go on a date with Jesus

Surely your goodness and love will follow me all the days of
my life, and I will dwell in the house of the LORD forever.

Psalm 23:6 (NIV)

Dream ~
. . . .

divinity
so fine…
blue gray
and white
perception
in my sight…
beautiful scene
uplifting
and carefree…
not certain
how or why
You made such
wonder for eyes
to see so high…
slow dancing
with You, Lord,
as clouds
drift by and by…
losing track of time
a blissful
poet's dream

The heavens declare the glory of God; the skies proclaim the work of his hands.

Psalm 19:1 (NIV)

Ever After ~

. . . .

happily, ever after twill be
living in
heaven with
resurrected
loves ones
set free
where every
chapter is
better
than the next
by God's grace
I know
that's what
awaits me
eternity
magnificent
eternity
happily, ever after twill be

For now we see only a reflection as in a mirror; then we shall
see face to face. Now I know in part; then I shall know fully,
even as I am fully known.

1 Corinthians 13:12 (NIV)

Faith ~
. . . .

grow
your faith
in the
valleys down
below
no need to
worry
how deep
they go
test
your faith
on the
mountain
so high
climb into
a zipline
and fly
fly
fly

But I have prayed for you, that your faith should not fail; and
when you have returned to Me, strengthen your brethren.

Luke 22:32 (NKJV)

Father of All ~

Lord
my heart
burns for You…
my soul
yearns for You…
for Your
affection…
for Your
direction…
Oh Lord how
I love You…
Holy
Holy
Holy
God of everything
Father to all
the Alpha
and the Omega
the beginning
and the end

I am the Alpha and the Omega, the First and the Last, the
Beginning and the End.

Revelation 22:13 (NIV)

Filter ~

. . . .

purify my heart
oh Lord
clean the filter
of my mind
keep my eyes
on You
fill me with
Your goodness
teach me
to discern
all that
pleases You
Lord show me
what to do
help me be
attuned
to all that
You've created...
may I
see You
with my heart

I LOVE YOU!

Blessed are the pure in heart, for they shall see God.

Matthew 5:8 (NKJV)

Flower ~
. . . .

delicate
as a
flower
beautiful as
can be
dear
loved one
you mean
the world
to me
your smile
is contagious
your eyes
light
up the room
please hurry
back to see me
really
really soon

Love one another as I have loved you

John 15:12 (NKJV)

Fruit of the Spirit ~

believers influenced
by Holy Spirit
are richly
filled within
sowing fruits of
LOVE
PEACE and
FAITHFULNESS
that stem from only Him
they walk and talk
just like folks do
while holding to
the nine virtues
with loving
GOODNESS
through and through
the closer you get
the more you find
there's nothing fake
or phony inside…
believers practice
SELF-CONTROL
allowing Holy Spirit
to take the lead role
KINDNESS,

GENTLENESS
and a helping hand
all play a part
in God's supernatural plan
don't take this wrong
believers aren't perfect
no human can be
but distinguishing
characteristics you see
believers have hope,
PATIENCE and
JOY...filled to the rim
overflowing within

But the fruit of the Spirit is love, joy, peace, longsuffering,
kindness, goodness, faithfulness, gentleness, self-control.
                                        Galatians 5:22-23 (NKJV)

Grace and Mercy ~

welcome to grace and mercy
you're always welcome here
where all things are forgiven
and God's love fills up the air

Let us then approach God's throne of grace with confidence,
so that we may receive mercy and find grace to help us in our
time of need.

Hebrews 4:16 (NIV)

Hallelujah ~

live like Jesus is coming
give thanks and
praise, praise, praise
live like Jesus is coming
Holy is His name
show grace
have mercy
He'll be here any moment
help others find their way
sing songs of
praise, praise, praise
live like Jesus is coming
He'll be here any moment
Hallelujah!
Hallelujah!

That He may establish your hearts without blame in holiness
before our God and Father at the coming of our Lord, Jesus.

1 Thessalonians 3:13 (NKJV)

Home Sweet Home ~

home sweet home
reflections
of beauty
and light
a slice of
heaven
on earth
where
everything's
nice…
a place
we long to be
so comforting
and free
welcome
to our home

Therefore welcome one another as Christ has welcomed you,
for the glory of God.

Romans 15:7 (ESV)

Hummingbird ~

hummingbird
hummingbird
let's
fly away
to a place
where there's
sweetness
and love in
the air…
lost in
the moment
it's suddenly
clear…it's
God's
omnipresence
I cherish
so dear

You will show me the path of life; In Your presence is fullness
of joy; At Your right hand are pleasures forevermore.

Psalm 16:11 (NKJV)

I Can ~

. . . .

I can
face the day
because
God accepted
me through
Christ…
I can
face the day
because
Jesus's death
and resurrection
gives me
forgiveness
and eternal life…
I can
face the day
because
God
loves me

We love because he first loved us.

1 John 4:19 (NIV)

I Love You ~

Jesus Christ
You are the way
You are the truth
I love You...
You are the Life
I come to You
I worship You
It's only You
I come to...
because of You
I have life
I have truth
through You and only You
You are the way
You are the truth
You are the life
Jesus Christ
I love You

Jesus said to him, "I am the way, the truth, and the life. No one comes to the Father except through me."

John 14:6 (NKJV)

Keepsake ~
. . . .

a promise
locked inside
my heart
a special keepsake
etched with
love…from
the mighty
mighty healer
life giver
master of
my heart…
receive
His promise…
believe it's true
etch His truth
on your heart too
He loves you…
with Jesus
you are
never alone
forever together
you'll be

I will never leave you nor forsake you.

Hebrews 13:5 (NKJV)

Kiss ~

. . . .

a perfect
bridegroom
waiting…
a love
so deep
so true…
kiss His Son
dear darling
He's passionate
for you…
walk with Him
talk with Him
praise His holy name…
consuming and renewing
His love remains
unchanged…
get intimate
and don't forget
to kiss His Son
dear darling

Kiss the Son, lest He be angry, And you perish in the way,
When His wrath is kindled but a little, Blessed are all those
who put their trust in Him.

Psalm 2:12 (NKJV)

Love Can Be ~

this
arguing
and fussing
is hurting
so many...
turn your
eyes on
Jesus
and see
what love
can be

Do not let your hearts be troubled.

John 14:1 (NIV)

Love God...Love People ~

check your
relationships often...
are you loving,
gentle and kind?
or self-centered,
harsh and blind?
take the blinders off...
spend more
time with
the Lord...
put Him
in first place
ask Him to
help you show
mercy and grace...
love God...
love people

Love is patient, love is kind. It does not envy, it does not boast, it is not proud. It does not dishonor others, it is not self-seeking, it is not easily angered, it keeps no record of wrongs. Love does not delight in evil but rejoices with the truth. It always protects, always trust, always hopes, always perseveres.

1 Corinthians 13:4-7 (NIV)

Love Her ~

cherish and honor
your wife
the same way
Christ loves you
start each day
brand new
tell her I love you
guard her
sensitive heart
be gentle, loving
and kind
hold her hand
and pray
ask about her day
your one flesh
bound together
and God's
the superglue
so feed your soul
with scripture
and keep His glue
with you... give thanks
and always consider
the woman
God gave to you

Husbands, likewise, dwell with them with understanding, giving honor to the wife, as to the weaker vessel, and as being heirs together of the grace of life, that your prayers may not be hindered

1 Peter 3:7 (NKJV)

Love Him ~

Respect
and love
your husband
it's written
and it's true
don't bother
trying to
change him
it's God's job
not for you…
prayer is
the best way
to lend
a helping hand
God's busy
working
through you
He has a
perfect plan

Be good wives to your husbands, responsive to their needs. There are husbands who, indifferent as they are to any words about God, will be captivated by your life of holy beauty. What matters is not your outer appearance—the styling of your hair, the jewelry you wear, the cut of your clothes—but your inner disposition.

1 Peter 3:1-4 (MSG)

Love Songs ~

. . . .

keep
singing
God's
love songs
He'll
dance
and sing
along
it's ok to
miss a beat
just find
God's rhythm
and tap
your feet
His heart
beats with
your tune

Sing to him, sing praise to him; tell of all his wonderful acts.
Psalm 105:2 (NIV)

Lovely Venue ~

transcendent above
dark sky star light…
suddenly blue
a lovely venue…
O sweet little bird
singing songs I do hear…
as pink hues touch blue
gently I rest in divine
immanence of God

In the beginning God created the heavens and the earth. The earth was without form, and void; and darkness was on the face of the deep. And the Spirit of God was hovering over the face of the waters. Then God said, "Let there be light" and there was light."

Genesis 1:1-3 (NKJV)

Next to You ~

. . . .

Jesus
wants your
heart…
not all
the things
you do…
He loves
you in
the morning…
and in
the afternoon…
and when
you go to bed
at night…
He's right
there next
to you

"Martha Martha" the Lord answered, "you are worried and
upset about many things, but few things are needed or indeed
only one. Mary has chosen what is better, and it will not be
taken away from her."

Luke 10:41-42 (NIV)

Promises ~

God's promises are true
over seven thousand to choose
read some everyday and
remember beloved
these covenants are written
to and for you
here's a few to view...

The Lord will fight for you; you need only be still.

Exodus 14:14 (NIV)

With joy you will draw water from the wells of salvation.

Isaiah 12:3 (NIV)

Therefore submit to God, resist the devil and he will flee from you.

James 4:7 (NKJV)

Share ~
· · · · · · · · · · · ·

day
by day
with God's grace
write love
notes
and tell
your
sweetheart
I love you…
dance
with her
in the
morning light…
give Him
a kiss
goodnight…
love is
meant to
share

Be devoted to one another in love. Honor one another above yourselves.

Romans 12:10 (NIV)

Supreme ~

my soul embraces Thee
who knows my heart complete
rejection has no hold
upon Thou greatness bold...
relationship supreme
contented mind set free

Jesus said to him. "You shall love your God with all your heart, with all your soul, and with all your mind.

Matthew 22:37 (NKJV)

The Golden Rule ~

follow
the golden rule...
be patient,
loving,
and kind...
give someone
your time...
help each other
love the other...
have mercy
and you'll see
what
Jesus gives
to you
and me

Do to others what you would have them do to you

Matthew 7:12 (NIV)

Upon a Rock ~

fear the Lord
with trembling hands
rejoice and
be made new…
in all your ways
acknowledge Him
He helps you
follow through…
delight in Him
share life with Him
make Him number
ONE!
give all the glory
of your story
to the Lord
so high…
mount upon a rock
and sing
His songs of praise
into the sky

Serve the Lord with fear, and rejoice with trembling.
Psalm 2:11 (NKJV)

You Are ~

. . . .

an original
make
and beauty…
you're one of
a kind
perfect in
God's eyes…
a blossom
of love
perfectly woven
together…
a masterpiece
mixed with
love, life, and
everything nice…
a gift from
the Lord
that's who
you are…

a heritage from the Lord, the fruit of the womb
Psalm 127:3 (NKJV)

PART TWO:

Encouragement

Anew You ~
. . . .

start each day
anew…
commit yourself
to God…
meditate
on scripture
and soon
you'll have
a mixture of
God's truth
deep inside…
here's a favorite
to keep in mind…

Charm is deceitful and beauty is vain, but a woman who
fears the Lord, she shall be praised (Proverbs 31:30, NASB)

find the time…
you'll surely shine
present yourself
anew…
become
the woman
God planned
for you!

Another Day ~

for when I go away
there will be another day
a chance to shine My light
hidden from eyesight
a holy holy light
I give to you My child
share My love
share My love
as white doves fly so free
tenderly with Me
for when I go away
there will be another day

Nevertheless I tell you the truth. It is to your advantage that
I go away; for if I do not go away, the Helper will not come
to you; but if I depart, I will send Him to you.

John 16:7 (KJV)

Ask ~
. . . .

don't
give up
on your
prayers
the Lord
is listening
Ask Him
Seek Him
Knock on His door…
pray more
and more
He opens
doors
don't give up
on your
prayers

Ask and it will be given to you; seek and you will find; knock and the door will be opened to you. For everyone who asks receives; the one who seeks finds; and the one who knocks, the door will be opened.

Matthew 7:7-8 (NIV)

Bible ~

. . . .

there's a scriptural
solution to all of
life's pollution…
look inside
The Bible
and find
God's truth…
no self help
book withstands
The Bible's
shelf life demand
or helps you
stand strong
when things
go wrong…
trust in
what God has
to say
get a bible today…
start solving
life's problems
God's perfect way

All your words are true; all your righteous laws are eternal.
Psalm 119:160 (NIV)

Calling ~

. . . .

prayer warrior
saint of saints
God's calling
out to you...
share the gospel
be an apostle
disciples
jump on board...
go out fish-in
there's just
no miss-in
God's people
come in shoals...
you've got the bait
so, don't be late
waiting on hot coals
go...spread the heat
or get cold feet
God's calling
out to you

He said to them "Go into all the world and preach the gospel
to all creation."

Mark 16:15 (NIV)

First Hour ~

give God
the first
hour
empowering
twill be
tis the
best way
to start
each day…
embodied in
God's temple
Holy Spirit
dwells
within…
share
the essence
of His presence
and the power
of first hour
transcends

Do you not know that you are God's temple and that God's
Spirit dwells in you?

1 Corinthians 3:16 (ESV)

Gift ~

. . . .

do what
God's called
you to do
He placed
a gift in you
take a leap
of faith
according
to His
grace

We have different gifts, according to the grace given to each
of us. If your gift is prophesying, then prophesy in accordance
with your faith; if it is serving, then serve; if it is teaching,
then teach; if it is encourage, then give encouragement; if it
is giving, then give generously; if it is to lead, do it diligently;
if it is to show mercy, do it cheerfully.

Romans 12:6-8 (NIV)

God Knots ~

. . . .

fear not…
don't get caught
in the enemies
plots and lies…
tie God knots
remember Daniel's friends
Shadrach, Meshach
and Abednego…
they entered
the blazing,
fiery furnace
never bowing down to
King Nebuchadnezzar's
idol of gold
they stood together
in spiritual faith
with the Lord by their
side…as He tied
a God knot
and brought
them out alive
fear not beloved…
a threefold cord is not quickly broken

                    Ecclesiastes 4:12 (NKJV)

Grace ~
. . . .

God's
not stuck
in yesterday
or tomorrow…
there's no
grace in
empty space…
now is
where
God's grace
is found

Grace to you and peace from God our Father and the Lord
Jesus Christ.

Philemon 1:3 (ESV)

Heaven's Door ~

great hope
we find in
Christ
through His
resurrected life…
death and sin
cannot defeat
believers…
who live a
faith-filled life
with glory
to the Lord
remembering
that one day
you'll walk through
heaven's door

His Lord said to him, "Well done, good and faithful servant;
you have been faithful over few things, I will make you ruler
over many things. Enter into the joy of the Lord."
Matthew 25: 23 (NKJV)

His Name ~

the heavens
declare
the glory of God
mighty is His
name…
better days will
surely come
stand tall,
be strong
walk in confidence
have **FAITH**
mighty is His
name…
better days will
surely come

For we walk by Faith, not by sight
2 Corinthians 5:7 (NKJV)

Host ~
· · · · · · · · · · ·

the sun
the moon
the stars...
angels near
and far...
heavenly
host of
God's
creation
serving
from afar
praise be
to the
Lord!

Praise the Lord! Praise the Lord from the heavens; Praise
Him in the heights! Praise Him, all His angels; Praise Him,
all His host! Praise Him, sun and moon; Praise Him, all you
stars of light!

Psalm 148: 1-3 (NKJV)

Home ~

. . . .

this is not
our home…
don't hold
tightly to this
world or the treasures
you store here…
feed your soul
with spiritual light…
keep eternity
in your site
and dear friend…
while your here
live a godly life
that's pleasing
to the Lord
this is not
our home…
it's a place
God's made
to spend our days
rejoicing in
His holy name…
be ready
He's coming any moment!

Friends, this world is not your home, so don't make yourselves cozy in it. Don't indulge your ego at the expense of your soul. Live an exemplary life in your neighborhood so that your actions will refute their prejudices. Then they'll be won over to God's side and be there to join the celebration when he arrives.

1 Peter 11-12 (MSG)

I Lack Nothing ~
. . . .

I love Jesus
and Jesus loves me
I lack nothing…
no aggravation
in relations
or problems
that confront
can take away
this love
I lack nothing…
no reason to
despair
or turn
and walk away
He's with me
night and day
and helps me
see the good
I lack nothing…

Fear the Lord, you his holy people, for those who fear him
lack nothing.

Psalm 34:9 (NIV)

I Wait for You, Lord ~

I wait in faith
I gain new strength
silent is my soul
Ahhh…
intimacy with Thee
no money can afford
I mount up with wings like an eagle
I run, I walk…never growing weary or weak
salvation, salvation, salvation
I wait for You, Lord!

But those who wait on the LORD shall renew *their* strength;
they shall mount up with wings like eagles, they shall run and
not be weary, they shall walk and not faint.

Isaiah 40:31 (NKJV)

I See ~

. . . .

to God's eternal glory
through gates of pearl I see
I walk on streets of gold
beauty made by Thee
a realm of natural wonders
so pure and life giving
while dancing in the breeze
the tree of life I see
no words can magnify
the spiritual truths inside
a glorified new body,
redeemed spirit set free
I see the perfect place
a magnificent holy city
where face to face I see…
The mighty mighty Savior
the Lord our God the King

For the wages of sin is death, but the gift of God is eternal life
in Christ Jesus our Lord.

Romans 6:23 (NIV)

Mirror ~

. . . .

the mirror can only
reveal a reflection
it can't even begin to
display how fearfully and
wonderfully God made you...
so remember the next time
you catch a glimpse
say these words out loud
mirror mirror on the wall
God created me
I'm beautiful, courageous
and strong

For you formed my inward parts; You covered me in my
mother's womb. I will praise You, for I am fearfully and wonderfully made. Marvelous are Your works And that my soul
knows very well.

Psalm 139:13-14 (NKJV)

Never Strays Away ~

God never strays away...
in His
perfect timing
He lights
the way...
He leads
the blind
to find
righteousness...
through
Christ
He molds
a simple life
redeeming lost souls
restoring broken hearts
to gates of pearl
and streets of gold...
God never strays away

God is our refuge and strength, an ever-present help in trouble.

Psalm 46:1 (NIV)

Old Made New ~

the old man's ways are gone
repents the old made new
God infused eternal life
redeemed spirit anew

Therefore, if anyone is in Christ, he is a new creation; old things have passed away; behold all things have become a new.

2 Corinthians 5:17 (NKJV)

Prayers ~

· · · · · · · · · · · · · ·

may
the prayers
that we
pray
rejoice
and praise
His name…
may
the words
that we
speak
be gracious
and give
peace

Rejoice always, pray continually, give thanks in all circumstances; for this is God's will for you in Christ Jesus.
1 Thessalonians 5:16-18 (NIV)

Road Map ~

walk with Him
talk with Him
meet Him
along the way
a road map
we can trust
day after day

The Lord delights in us, then He will bring us into this land
and give it to us, a land which flows with milk and honey
                                    Numbers 14:8 (NKJV)

Salt & Light ~

. . . .

Sugar and spice are nice
but it's salt that seasons
the earth and light
that brightens the world...
be a shining star
glow wherever you go
helping others see
how bright
God's light can be...
bring your salt-filled life
shake it everywhere
flavor all God's people
with tender love and care
Jesus said...
"you are salt of the earth...you are the light in the world"
that's who you are
filled with salt and light...
changing lives
through Jesus Christ
(Matthew 5:13-14, NIV)

Shadow ~

Shadow of me
Shadows of trees
Sunny days and silhouettes
She walks with strength and dignity
Laughing at the future

She is clothed with strength and dignity, and she laughs without fear of the future.

Proverbs 31:25(NLT)

Sharpen ~
. . . .

when
a friend
needs a hand
take a stand…
sharpen
one another
with the swords
of the spirit…
inerrant is
God's word…
minister
with love and
compassion too
helping one
another
the way
Holy Spirit
helps you

the sword of the spirit, which is God's word
Ephesians 6:17 (NIV)

As iron sharpens iron, So a man sharpens the countenance
of his friend
Proverbs 27:17 (NKJV)

Soul Print ~

. . . .

a footprint
in the sand
doesn't
last forever
but the
soul print
of God's love
never
fades away
He's with you
night and day
so never lose
hope…
never ever
lose hope!

We have this hope as an anchor for the soul.
Hebrews 6:19 (NIV)

Sweet Eternity ~

. . . .

come join
sweet eternity
you're always
welcome here…
where life goes
on forever
and God's grace
fills up the air…
you'll hit
a home run
darling and slide
into home base…
the crown
of life awaits
you when
you put
Christ in
first place…
come join
sweet eternity
your always welcome here

I write these things to you who believe in the name of the
Son of God so that you may know that you have eternal life.
1 John 5:13 (NIV)

Sun, Moon, & Stars ~

sun, sun shining sun
the day has just begun
God's greater light
divides the night
now let's go have some fun...
moon, moon great big moon
I need to go home soon
God placed this night light
in my sight, I'll start
my chart by noon...
stars, stars so many stars
look at the stars tonight
and rest knowing
God's bright little lights
twinkle through the night...

God spoke: "Lights! Come out! Shine in Heaven's sky! Separate Day from Night. Mark seasons and days and years, Lights in Heaven's sky to give light to Earth." And there it was.

Genesis 1:14-15 (MSG)

Stones & Butterflies ~

Jesus hold me just like
You held me before
You take small **Faith**
and make it bigger…
like the butterfly effect
You flap small wings
and make **Change** bigger…
like the seed embryo
You plant small things
and make **Life** bigger…
like the ripples from a stone
thrown into a pond
You throw small stones
and make **Hope** bigger…
Jesus hold me just like
You held me before
You take small **Faith**
and make it bigger…

I'll flap small wings
I'll plant seedlings
I'll sing Your songs
I'll throw gemstones into Your pond
I'll make **Faith** bigger
Lord help me make **Faith** bigger

Because you have so little faith. Truly I tell you, if you have faith as small as a mustard seed, you can say to this mountain,' Move from here to there' and it will move. Nothing will be impossible for you.

Matthew 17:20 (NIV)

Today ~

let
the Lord
be your
guide
on this
magic
carpet ride
SEE the sun bursting through and the flowers as they bloom
HEAR the birds as they sing hallelujah in God's name
SMELL the jasmine in the air as it floats through your hair
TOUCH the turf or go surf on this magic carpet ride
and don't
forget
along
the way
to thank
God
for this
beautiful day!

This is the day the Lord has made Let us rejoice and be glad
in it.

Psalm 118:24 (ESV)

Wildest Dreams ~

thank you,
Holy Spirit for
living
inside me…
a helper
Jesus gave
that's
beyond
my wildest
dreams…
grateful
to be living
in peace
and harmony
with the
Holy Spirit
who teaches
all good things

But the Helper, the Holy Spirit, whom the Father will send in My name, He will teach you all things, and bring to your remembrance all things that I have said to you. Peace I leave with you, My peace I give to you; not as the world gives do I give to you. Let not your heart be troubled, neither let it be afraid.

John 14:26-27 (NASB)

PART THREE:

Long Suffering

Amends ~
. . . .

forgive
one
another
as your
heavenly
Father
forgives
you...
we are
all guilty
of sin
repent,
forgive
and
make
amends
God loves
us all
Amen!

For if you forgive other people when they sin against you,
your heavenly Father will also forgive you. But if you do not
forgive others theirs sins, your Father will not forgive your
sins.

Matthew 6:14-15 (NIV)

Angels & Demons ~

Locked inside with demons
frozen by despair
hiding from reality
thinking no one cares
monsters they surround me
tucked deep in secret spots
waiting to devour and
take my aching heart
certain I can handle
these demons that I hide
craving after craving
not certain I'll survive
who knows when they'll take me
I'll take my chances now
was I ever sober? was I even there?
I'm sorry that I left you
I'm sorry that you cared
my heart is finally resting
the demons I left there
angels now surround me
my body made brand new
I'll see you when you get here… I love you to the moon!

The Lord is my Shepard I shall not want

Psalm 23:1 (NKJV)

Apostle ~

. . . .

God's word
tells us His grace
and strength
are sufficient
and made perfect
in weakness
so why do we
complain when
the going get's tough?
the Apostle Paul
managed hour by hour
to preach the gospel…
whether abounding
in plenty or left
with none…
in ALL circumstances
he boasted in the
power of Christ
Can we do this too?

And He said to me, "My grace is sufficient for you, for My
strength is made perfect in weakness." Therefore most gladly
I will rather boast in my infirmities, that the power of Christ
may rest upon me.

2 Corinthians 12:9 (NKJV)

89

Beatitudes ~

. . . .

beloved cleanse your soul…
give your whole heart to God…
follow Jesus Christ's
standard of conduct…
meditate on the beatitudes

Blessed are the poor in spirit, for theirs is the kingdom of heaven.
Blessed are those who mourn, for they shall be comforted.
Blessed are the meek, for they shall inherit the earth.
Blessed are those who hunger and thirst for righteousness, for they shall be satisfied.
Blessed are the merciful, for they shall receive mercy.
Blessed are the pure in heart, for they shall see God.
Blessed are the peacemakers, for they shall be called sons of God.
Blessed are those who are persecuted for righteousness sake, for theirs is the kingdom of heaven.

Matthew 5:3-10 (NKJV)

Bite ~

· · · · · · · · · ·

instant gratification comes with a price…
remember when Eve
took the fruit from the tree?
she didn't think twice
before taking a bite
and gave some to Adam too…
so before you bite off
more than you can chew…
seek God's advice
He's always with you!

And they heard the Lord God walking in the garden in the
cool of the day and Adam and his wife hid themselves from
the presence of the Lord God among the trees of the garden.
Genesis 3:8 (NKJV)

Captive ~
. . . .

held captive in
darkness and sin
living life at wit's end?
cry out to the Lord...
sin no more...
praise Him...trust Him
His mercies are brand new
each day for me and you...
He forgives ALL sins
He makes the darkness tremble
live the rest of your life
filled with His greatness
and light...

He calms the storm so that its waves are still
                        Psalms 107:29 (NKJV)

Cross ~
. . . .

taking
up the cross
and following
the Lord
requires losing
the false
illusion of
one's self
only to find
the God grown
authentic
self

Then Jesus said to His disciples, "If anyone desires to come after Me, let him deny himself, and take up his cross, and follow Me. For whoever desires to save his life will lose it, but whoever loses his life for My sake will find it."

Matthew 16:24-25 (NKJV)

Dance ~

. . . .

when you can...
let go of what you've lost
dance in what you have...
pay attention where your mind dwells...
stop losing time in the spells of the past
take your brokenness and
shine some light for Jesus...
life is so much brighter
when you dance in what you have

Summing it all up, friends, I'd say you'll do best by filling
your minds and meditating on things true, noble, reputable,
authentic, compelling, gracious—the best, not the worst; the
beautiful, not the ugly; things to praise, not things to curse.
Do that, and God, who makes everything work together, will
work you into his most excellent harmonies.

Philippians 4:8-9 (MSG)

Dark Pathways ~

. . . .

on dark
pathways
that I run
there are
crossroads,
fog and mud…
through
the shadow
of life's death
You help me
catch my
breath…
You comfort me
You never leave
You keep my foot
from slipping…
I fear not
even tripping…
on dark
pathways
that I run

Your word is a lamp for my feet, a light on my path.

Psalm 119:105 (NIV)

Deliver ~

serve God
wherever
you are…
be content
His love's
legit…
pray
fervently
and trust that
God is
omnipotent
be faithful
and obedient…
God will
deliver you!

He delivers and rescues, And He works signs and wonders
In heaven and on earth, Who has delivered Daniel from the
power of the Lions.

Daniel 6:27 (NKJV)

Devil's Brew ~
. . . .

don't get caught
in the devil's
brew
and fall
through
deep dark
cracks…
stop sinking
while your
time
still lasts…
you know
the way…
God's tried
and true
don't get caught in
the devils
brew

Be alert and of sober mind, your enemy the devil prowls
around like a roaring lion looking for someone to devour.
Resist him, standing firm in the faith, because you know that
the family of believers throughout the world is undergoing
the same kind of sufferings.

1 Peter 5:8-9 (NIV)

Ego ~
. . . .

let go of your ego
stop edging God out
pride goes before a fall, y'all
humility is strength under control
suffer a while
it's not futile
it's all for the good
you will see when you believe!

Pride goes before destruction, a haughty spirit before a fall.

Proverbs 16:18 (NIV)

Enduring ~

it's not
what life
looks like
it's what we
see in
Jesus
that provides
a better way
from
temptation
as we
stray

No temptation has overtaken you except what is common to mankind. And God is faithful; he will not let you be tempted beyond what you can bear. But when you are tempted, he will also provide a way out so that you can endure it.

1 Corinthians 10:13 (NIV)

Freedom ~

. . . .

in keeping
God's
great laws
true freedom
I have found…
allowing
God's temple
to lovingly
abound…
there's no guilt
in His laws
only forgiveness
and peace
to comfort
my afflictions
as His servant
I am free

Stand fast therefore in the liberty by which Christ has made
us free and do not be entangled again with a yoke of bondage.
Galatians 5:1 (NKJV)

Glory ~
. . . .

I threw away
my enemies
the skeletons
are gone
God granted me
SERENITY the
COURAGE
to move on
WISDOM only
God supplies
and multiply He does
Redeemer
of my story
Glory! Glory! Glory!

God grant me the Serenity to accept the things I cannot change the Courage to change the things I can and the Wisdom to know the difference.

Serenity Prayer

Heart ~
. . . .

be patient in the heartache
greater things are yet to come...
the suffering and pain
are wrapped in God's great love...
the joy you'll soon experience
when the air is finally clear
reminds us of a scripture
a truth you need to hear...
Consider that our present sufferings are not worth comparing
with the glory that will be revealed in us (Romans 8:18, NIV)
remember this great truth
and promise that God made
the next time that your heart
is broken or in pain

Hope ~

. . . .

all I want to do
is what pleases You…
my hope is in You Jesus
my hope is in You God…
when I fall short as I often do
Lord help me look to You…
Father hold onto me tight
through the day
and through the night…
safe and sound in Your arms
is where I long to be…
I'll shelter into place
as You fill up empty space…
comforting my soul
so gracious is Your love…
all I want to do
is what pleases You…
my hope is in You Jesus
my hope is in You God…
when I fall short as I often do
Lord help me look to You…

For all have sinned and fall short of the glory of God.
Romans 3:23 (NIV)

Humble Heart ~

God loves
a humble
heart…
break free
from all
barriers of
pride…keep
your heart
wide open…
be grateful,
kind
and humble…
find joy
in humility…
abiding
in His love

Blessed are the poor in spirit, for theirs is the kingdom of heaven.

Matthew 5:3 (NIV)

Pride goes before destruction, and a haughty spirit before a fall. Better to be of a humble spirit with the lowly, than to divide the spoil with the proud.

Proverbs 16:18-19 (NKJV)

Indeed ~
. . . .

there's so much more to life
than seeking worldly gifts and pleasures
these things we leave behind
only emptiness to find
make a change today
serve God each and everyday...
great gain we find in indeed

Now godliness with contentment is great gain. For we brought nothing into this world, and it is certain we can carry nothing out.

1 Timothy 6:6-7 (NKJV)

Like Jesus ~

. . . .

walk and talk like Jesus
it's simple if you try
keeping up the rhythm
is the challenge that we find...
turn your heart towards people
help the lady with the door
say excuse me in the store
thank the clerk who's at work...
give up your space in line
be patient all the time
give your heart to Jesus
He helps you keep the rhythm
and gives you all the wisdom...
don't waste another minute
go walk and talk like Jesus

Each of you should use whatever gift you have received to serve others, as faithful stewards of God's grace in its various forms. If anyone speaks, they should do so as one who speaks the very words of God. If anyone serves, they should do so with the strength God provides, so that in all things God may be praised through Jesus Christ. To him be the glory and the power forever and ever Amen.

1 Peter 4:10-11 (NIV)

More ~

. . . .

stuck in self wanting something else
that I really don't need... always
trying to ease this feeling taunting me
this constant want does not heed
Your truth, Your word, Your peace
self soothing for these things
has left me wanting more...
my bank account I watch as I
search for more, more, more
these things I cannot hide
as their always by my side...
irritation in relations
always wanting more
Lord help me want You more
and give away the hoard

Jesus said to him, "If you want to be perfect, go sell what
you have and give to the poor, and you will have treasure
in heaven; and come follow Me." But when the young man
heard that saying, he went away sorrowful, for he had great
possessions.

Matthew 19:21-22 (NKJV)

Sin No More ~

no matter
what
you've
done…
it's never
too late
to **go**
and sin
no more…

Jesus said, "Neither do I condemn you; go and sin no more."
John 8:11 (NKJV)

Soar ~
. . . .

if it isn't
one thing
it's
another
but those
who hope
in the
Lord
will
spread
their wings
and soar,
soar,
soar

But those who hope in the Lord will renew their strength.
They will soar on wings like eagles; they will run and not
grow weary, they will walk and not grow faint.

Isaiah 40:31 (NIV)

Stop, Drop, and Pray ~

spread too thin
need rest within
struggling
through this life
stop drop and pray
meditate God's way...
find the good book
It's sure to hook
the title is the Bible...
scripture is a mixture
a proven recipe
that guards your hearts
through Jesus
just open up and see

Be anxious for nothing, but in everything by prayer and sup-
plication with thanksgiving let your request be known to
God; and the peace of God which surpasses all understanding will guard your hearts and minds through Christ Jesus.

Philippians 4:6-7 (NKJV)

Thorns ~

· · · · · · · · · · · · · ·

the consequences hit
like a ton of bricks
why did this happen to me
just wanted a quick fix
grateful God's so patient
and waiting in the midst
free will equals choices
and consequences stick…
thank you, God, for working
all things for the good
even when I do things
I know I never should
these thorns that I've gathered
remain in my side
and may be just the blessing
I've needed all this time

And we know that in all things God works for the good of
those who love him, who have been called according to his
purpose.

Romans 8:28 (NIV)

Wait ~
· · · · · · · · · ·

I wait for You Lord
with surrendered will...
no eye has seen
or can perceive
the preparations,
the divine blessings
no ear has heard
or deserves such gifts
I wait for You Lord...
with sincerity of heart
from the start
it's only been You

For since the beginning of the world men have not heard nor
perceived by ear, not has the eye seen any God besides you,
who acts for the one who waits for Him.

Isaiah 64:4 (NKJV)

PART FOUR:

Truth

Abide ~

. . . .

abide in
Thee vine
while
Thy sap
seeks
to find
thine
branches
abiding
in Thee...
Thou soon
will produce
divine
blossoms
of fruit
that cometh
from root
of His
love

Abide in Me, and I in you. As the branch cannot bear fruit
of itself, unless it abides in the vine, neither can you, unless
you abide in Me.

John 15:4 (NKJV)

Atone ~
. . . .

God alone
has shown me how to trust
I must confess
my life's a mess without Him
He's sown my broken pieces
and placed me at His feet
repeat, repeat, repeat...

God alone
TRULY
knows my heart
He never condones
or is shocked by what
He sees
He loves me...

God alone
goes with me wherever I go
I'm never alone
atone, atone, atone

Growing in the Lord!

Behavior ~

have you
checked your
behavior lately?
it's most important
that you do…
repent dear friend…
confess your sins
and set God's word
as your standard
of living…
there is no
better time
to get right…
fix your eyes
on Jesus…
fill up with
peace and light
follow through
God's people are watching you

In everything set them an example by doing what is good. In teaching show integrity, seriousness and soundness of speech that cannot be condemned, so that those who oppose you may be ashamed because they have nothing bad to say about us.

Titus 2:7-8 (NIV)

Beware ~

beware of false prophets
who minimize Christ
by glorifying life through
power, wealth and lies...
it's a shameful way indeed
filled with vanity and greed
these posers soon lose the chance
to dance in God's great truth

Watch out for false prophets. They come to you in sheep's clothing, but inwardly they are ferocious wolves. By their fruit you will recognize them. Do people pick grapes from thornbushes, or figs from thistles? Likewise, every good tree bears good fruit, but a bad tree bears bad fruit. A good tree cannot bear bad fruit, and a bad tree cannot bear good fruit, Every tree that does not bear good fruit is cut down and thrown into the fire. Thus by their fruit you will recognize them.

Matthew 7:15-20 (NIV)

Christian ~

I am a Christian
with great
strength and control
forever in His grace…
and I humbly
wear a badge of honor
bestowed by
the Lord

Blessed are the meek, For they shall inherit the earth.

Matthew 5:5 (NKJV)

Done ~

. . . .

on a great,
great day
we will see
on display
how godless
this world's become…
flames of fire will
be to all ye
refusing belief
in His Son
who sits by His side
providing much time…
God the Father,
God the Son and
God the Holy Spirit
three equals ONE…
the godless ruler convicted…
it's DONE!

And when He has come, He will convict the world of sin,
and of righteousness, and of judgement: of sin, because they
do not believe in Me; of righteousness, because I go to My
Father and you see Me no more; of judgement, because the
ruler of this world is judged.

John 16:8-11 (NKJV)

Fear Not
. . . .

fear not, fear not, fear not
the angel of the Lord declares
be of good, good, good cheer
bring your burdens and your cares
for the Lord has overcome
fear not, fear not, fear not
the Lord has overcome!

Then the angel said to them, "Do not be afraid, for behold,
I bring you good tidings of great joy which will be to all
people. For there is born to you this day in the city of David
a Savior, who is Christ the Lord. And this will be a sign to
you: You will find a Babe wrapped in swaddling cloths, lying
in a manger."

Luke 2:10-12 (NKJV)

Flee ~
· · · · · · · · · ·

yield
to Thee
who makes
crooked things straight
and the lost see
done in secret space
away from prying eyes
His mighty deeds
no one hides or
can truly flee...
the master guides
you see?
Omnipresent is Thee

Where can I go from your Spirit? Where can I flee from your presence? If I go up to the heavens, you are there; if I make my bed in the depths, you are there. If I rise on the wings of the dawn, if I settle on the far side of the sea, even there your hand will guide me, your right hand will hold me fast. If I say, "Surely the darkness will hide me and the light become night around me, "even the darkness will not be dark to you; the night will shine like the day, for darkness is as light to you.

Psalm 139:7-12 (NIV)

Flesh ~

release the flesh that gives no rest
enjoy a spirit filled life...
take every thought captive with
obedience to Christ...
you will be amazed at the difference
His truth makes in and through
your life... eliminate the toxins
don't conform to this world
be transformed by the Lord
activate God's word at
the door of your mind...
don't speculate, meditate... focus on what's true, honorable
and right...
renew your mind each day
emulate His way

For those that live according to the flesh set their minds on
the things of the flesh, but those who live according to the
Spirit, the things of the Spirit.

Romans 8:5 (NKJV)

Grow ~

. . . .

God
doesn't always
shout here's
the easiest route...
He let us
grow instead...
God loves
you so much
that He gave
His one and
only Son
to save us
from all trials
to come...
dear loved one
water your
soul with Jesus
and overflow
with blossoms
of His love...
God grows beautiful things

Grow in the grace and knowledge of our Lord and Savior
Jesus Christ. To Him be glory both now and forever! Amen.

2 Peter 3:18 (NKJV)

King ~
· · · · · · · · · · ·

revere
the Lord…
fear
the Lord…
the
mighty
King
of Kings…
there
is no
higher power
than
the Lord
our God
the
King!

Let every soul be subject unto the higher powers. For there is
no power but of God: the powers that are ordained of God.

Romans 13:1 (NKJV)

Noah ~

· · · · · · · · · · ·

once upon
the sins of man
God rained down
His great wrath
flooding fleshly paths
only few lives did He spare…
Noah had God's grace
for he was faithful and obedient
and on the day
the flood came
God saved his family
including the ingredients
for future life to be…
much is left to say
but I'll leave
you here to ponder
all the reasons why
faith in Christ is power
and in the last hour
how grateful twill be
when Jesus saves us from
the wrath of man we see

Noah did everything just as God commanded him.

Genesis 6:22 (NIV)

125

Oneness ~
. . . .

oneness
is found
in unity
with Spirit…
beautifully
designed with
peace in mind…
always gentle
and loving…
a faithful bond
to keep…
sweet harmony
we reap

Be completely humble and gentle; be patient, bearing with one another in love. Make every effort to keep the unity of the Spirit through the bond of peace. There is one body and one Spirit, just as you were called; one Lord, one faith, one baptism; one God and Father of all, who is over all and through all and in all.

Ephesians 4:2-6 (NIV)

Open Your Eyes ~

the grass
isn't
greener on
the other side…
can you not
see the value
where you are?
you don't have
to go far…
open your eyes
simply open
your eyes…
if you're looking
for a better life
look no more…
you've got Christ!

The Lord is my Shepard; I shall not want. He makes me to lie
down in green pastures; He leads me beside the still waters.
He restores my soul; He leads me in the paths of righteousness for His name sake.

Psalm 23:1-3 (NKJV)

Overflow ~
. . . .

stop spending
time with
negativity…
focus on
the good
and all
the blessings…
the Lord
your
mighty Savior
came and set
you free…
let your life
overflow
with
positivity

For as a he thinketh in his heart so is he…

Proverbs 23:7 (KJV)

You prepare a table before me in the presence of my enemies;
You anoint my head with oil, my cup runs over.

Psalm 23: 5 (NKJV)

Poke Around ~

it's up to you to choose
the cards that win or lose...
don't poke around with sin my friend
the devil is a joker...
he'll pull out all the cards
and let you win a hand or two
until he finds your ace...
he'll cut you loose
with a tight fitting noose and
watch his plan win hand after hand...
God dealt you the WINNING hand
when He gave His only Son
to save you from the joker's run...
it's up to you to choose the cards
that win or lose...
don't poke around with sin my friend
the devil is a joker

The thief comes only to steal and kill and destroy; I have
come that they may have life, and have it to the full.

John 10:10 (NIV)

Priceless ~

in the furnace
of affliction
God turns up
the heat of
the soul
but after all
the toll
is priceless!

Come to Me, all you who labor and are heavy laden, and I
will give you rest. Take my yoke upon you and learn from
Me, for I am gentle and lowly in heart, and you will find rest
for your souls.

Matthew 11: 28-30 (NKJV)

Reconciled ~

help one
another
find faith
and peace
on earth...
you have been
reconciled for
God's good
by the blood
of His Son...
where harmonious
unity is found
and love abounds...
be a peacemaker

Blessed are the peacemakers, for they shall be called sons of
God.

Matthew 5:9 (ESV)

Righteousness Sake ~

stand up
brothers and sisters
in Christ
enough is enough...
sanctify the Lord
your God in your Heart...
be ready to give
an answer for the hope
that lives in you (1 Peter 3:15, NKJV)
speak up for
righteousness sake...
verbalize your faith...
show strength
and confidence...
Lord help us
stand for You
while suffering
through this
life reminding us
that one day
all will be just right

Blessed are those who are persecuted for righteousness' sake,
for theirs is the kingdom of heaven.

Matthew 5:3-10 (NKJV)

Rock ~

. . . .

the sins of man
reach far and wide
they know
no boundaries
and cannot hide…
it's up to you beloved
to break generational curses…
study bible verses and be the
man God planned…
Fear the Lord
Revere the Lord
Lead your family…
build your house on rock
no aftershock can mock
pray together, stay together
plant spiritual seeds
and grow, grow, grow,
in Christ abundantly

"For I know the plans I have for you," declares the Lord,
"plans to prosper you and not to harm you, plans to give you
hope and a future."

Jeremiah 29:11 (NIV)

Saved ~

. . . .

covered
by
His
blood
and
saved
through
His love…
truth
and grace
remain
unchanged

Jesus Christ is the same yesterday, today, and forever.

Hebrews 13:8 (NIV)

Suffering ~
. . . .

it's only here
with Jesus
the suffering is
not in vain...
hold on in
the midst
and focus on
God's reign

The Lord your God in your midst, The Mighty One, will save; He will rejoice over you with gladness, He will quiet you with His love, He will rejoice over you with singing.

Zephaniah 3:17 (NKJV)

The Way ~

the way the truth & the life
is yours to choose...
but only through
the mighty Savior Jesus Christ...
God sent His only Son
to walk among mankind and
save us from the wrath
and sins of fallen time...
Christ took the fall
He paid the price, redeemed
us all... He sacrificed...
believe in Him, trust in Him
make Him your Lord Savior...
confess your sins
repent dear friend
make the choice today...
the pathway is quite narrow but
the gate is straight ahead...
it's easy to get sidetracked
so don't delay... let's pray

For God so loved the world that He gave His only begot-
ten Son, that whoever believes in Him should not perish but
have everlasting life.

John 3:16 (NIV)

There Goes I ~

have
you
gossiped
or been
judgmental
lately?
beloved
don't
do this…
have
empathy
open your
heart and
say…
but for the grace of God, **there goes I…**

Do not judge, or you too will be judged. For in the same way you judge others, you will be judged, and with the measure you use, it will be measured to you.

Matthew 7:1-2 (NIV)

Thou Art ~
. . . .

shadows of love
drifting above
limitless is Thee
the world is but a speck…
no one can fathom
how great Thou art indeed

Great is the LORD, and greatly to be praise; And His greatness is unsearchable.

Psalm 145:3 (NKJV)

Three Hearts ~

three hearts came together
in desperate times of need
where loyalty met truth
bringing forth a mighty king

Naomi, Ruth, and Boaz
three hearts with God in mind
beautiful relationships
and brokenness inside

through time the greatest
blessing of love
and faith in God
came our mighty Savior
the Lord our God His Son

Where you go I will go, and where you stay I will stay
                                        Ruth 1:16 (NIV)

Treasures ~

treasures
and fortune
on earth
gain
nothing
eternally
and have
no lasting
legacy...
indeed
a heart
that hopes
in Jesus
overflows
eternally
leaving
a heritage
of faith a
lasting
legacy

For where your treasure is, there your heart will be also.
Matthew 6:21 (NIV)

Two Sins ~
· · · · · · · · · · · · · · · · ·

you've heard it said before
two wrongs don't make a right
pride and ignorance don't win a fight
payback is a sin
the devil dives right in
he'll fool you into all the reasons
paybacks how you win...
God strength is what you need
to right the wrong is victory...
don't let the devil fool you
fear the Lord, revere the Lord
throw away the sin
this is how you win...
two sins don't make a right

But I say to you who hear: Love your enemies, do good to
those who hate you, bless those who curse you, and pray for
those who spitefully use you.

Luke 6:27-28 (NKJV)

Truth ~
. . . .

stumbling morally
misaligned?
pursuits of truth to find?
mortality lurks near by
as questions plaque the mind
all answers held by root
in the origin of God's truth

All Scripture is given by inspiration of God, and is profitable
for doctrine, for reproof, for correction, for instruction in
righteousness.

2 Timothy 3:16 (NKJV)

Understanding ~

. . . .

God's understanding
is higher than ours
no need to bang or hang
your head
this verse will help you
trust His plan
"Trust in the Lord with All your heart, and lean not on your
own understanding in all your ways acknowledge Him and
He shall direct your paths" (Proverbs 3:5-6, NKJV)
some things
are better left alone
discernment comes from
the one on the throne
you'll understand more as you
lean on the Lord His ways are
sometimes mysteries
no worries for you and me
we'll see someday in eternity

"For My thoughts are not your thoughts, Nor are your ways
My ways," says the LORD.
"For as the heavens are higher than the earth, So are My ways
higher than your ways,
And My thoughts than your thoughts."

Isaiah 55:8-9 (NKJV)

Warfare ~

heaven and hell lucifer fell
a spiritual battle begins
there is no time to rest
get dressed in your best
pick up the sword of the Spirit...
keep a watchful eye and
stay far away from sin
you are a prayer warrior...
the devil competes
through cunning deceit
prowling like a lion...
the power in the fight
comes from a praying warrior
who prays with all their might
the warfare marches on

The thief comes only to steal and kill and destroy; I have
come that they may have life, and have it to the full.

John 10:10 (NIV)

Finally, be strong in the Lord and in his mighty power. Put
on the full armor of God, so that you can take your stand
against the devil's schemes.

Ephesians 6:10-11 (NIV)

Be sober, be vigilant; because your adversary the devil walks
about like a roaring lion, seeking whom he may devour.

1 Peter 8 (NKJV)

What Is Right ~

are we
getting used
to the dark?
impurities
constantly
in our sight…
immoral life's
crossing lines
ending in
destruction…
dangerous passions
darkening light
evil desires
will never
be right…
put these sins
to death…
enlighten your life
by doing
what is right…
turn away from sin!

For the wages of sin is death, but the gift of God is eternal life
in Christ Jesus our Lord.

Romans 6:23 (NIV)

Wisdom ~
. . . .

seek God's
wisdom
in all
you do
heed His
warnings and
promptings too...
Holy Spirit
lives in you
so open up
the mind
and discernment
you shall find

If any of you lacks wisdom, let him ask God who gives to all
liberally and without reproach, and it will be given to him.

James 1:5 (NKJV)

What Pleases Him Will Please You Too ~

find your purpose in life
through glorifying Christ…
He gave His life for you
this gift of love to use
to help change people's lives
and make a difference too…
take up the cross
show God gratitude
what pleases Him will please you too
have no fear Holy Spirit
is always there… a guiding light indeed
find your purpose in life
by glorifying Christ…
this is what you were born to do

Whatever you do, do it all for the glory of God.
1 Corinthians 10:31 (NIV)

Words ~

words
mean a lot
especially
to God
every
single word
reveals
conditions
of the heart

Out of the same mouth come praise and cursing. My brothers and sisters, this should not be.

James 3:10 (NIV)

Conclusion

. . . .

Believe it or not, God loves us even more than our closest loved ones do. Along with this unsurpassed love, He offers us a choice to accept His Son, Jesus Christ, as our personal Savior, and by doing so, we share in the union of the Godhead Trinity and promise of eternal life. Why would we live life without the supernatural divinity of God the Father, God the Son, and God the Holy Spirit?

It is in your absolute best interest to put on the whole armor of God, otherwise you will be continually defeated by strongholds, setbacks and most of all, where will your hope come from? The devil builds a threating powerbase that preys on weak links meant to kill, steal, and destroy. Keep in mind we fight against the devil's schemes in this fallen world, not one another. We are living in spiritual warfare friend, be prepared and start shielding against the evil ones blazing fiery darts. Protect yourself and others with great faith. Accept Jesus Christ as your personal Savior today. Your life depends on it.

He who is in you is greater than he who is in the world.

1 John 4 (NKJV)

Acknowledgements

All the glory belongs to God almighty!
Thank You, Lord, for allowing me to glorify You.

I love You,
Ruth

Bibliography

· · · · · · · · · · · · · · · · · · ·

Sifton, Elisabeth. 2003. *The serenity prayer: faith and politics in times of peace and war*. New York: Norton.

CPSIA information can be obtained
at www.ICGtesting.com
Printed in the USA
BVHW091528220521
607798BV00007B/761